History of Vermont Civil War Regiments

Artillery, Cavalry, and Infantry

Christopher Cox

© 2013 Christopher Cox
ISBN: 978-1492818762

Dedicated To
The 5,224 Vermont Boys that paid
The ultimate sacrifice for the cause of the Union

Table of Contents

1st Company Heavy Artillery 1

1st Battery Light Artillery 2

2nd Battery Light Artillery 3

3rd Battery Light Artillery 4

1st Cavalry 5

1st Infantry 8

2nd Infantry 10

3rd Infantry 12

4th Infantry 14

5th Infantry 16

6th Infantry 18

7th Infantry 20

8th Infantry 22

9th Infantry 24

10th Infantry 26

11th Infantry (1st Heavy Artillery) 28

12th Infantry (9 Months) 30

13th Infantry (9 Months) 32

14th Infantry (9 Months) 34

15th Infantry (9 Months) 36

16th Infantry (9 Months) 38

17th Infantry 40

18th Infantry 42

Bibliography 43

1st Company Heavy Artillery

- History
    - Mustered In
        - April, 1865 Port Hudson, La
    - Mustered Out
        - July 25, 1865
- Total Enrollment
    - 118 Men
- Organization
    - Organized April, 1865, from surplus Recruits of 2nd Vermont Battery Light Artillery.
    - Duty at Port Hudson, La., until July, 1865.
    - Moved to Vermont July 7-20.
- Battles
    - N/A
- Officers
    - Captain Henry W. Fales
    - First Lieutenant Martin Peil
    - Second Lieutenant William W. Kasson
- Died of Disease
    - 4 Men
- Discharged for Disability
    - 7 Men
- Suicide
    - 1 Man

1st Battery Light Artillery

- History
    - Mustered In
        - February 18, 1862, Brattleboro
    - Mustered Out
        - August 10, 1864
- Total Enrollment
    - 217 Men
- Killed in Action
    - 1 Man
- Died of Wounds
    - 2 Men
- Died of Disease
    - 42 Men
- Died by Accident
    - 1 Man

- Organization
    - Organized at Brattleboro and mustered in February 18, 1862.
    - Left State for New York City March 6.
    - Sailed on Steamer "Wallace" for Ship Island March 10, arriving April 5.
    - Attached to Phelps' 1st Brigade, Dept. of the Gulf, to December, 1862.
    - Artillery, 2nd Division, 19th Army Corps, Dept. of the Gulf, to June, 1863.
    - Artillery, 3rd Division, 19th Army Corps, to September, 1863.
    - Artillery, District of LaFourche, Dept. of the Gulf, to January, 1864.
    - Artillery, 2nd Division, 19th Army Corps, Army of the Gulf, to July, 1864.
    - Artillery, 1st Division, 19th Army Corps, to August, 1864.
    - Recruits transferred to 2nd Vermont Battery.

- Battles
    - Plain's Store
    - Siege of Port Hudson
    - Pleasant Hill
    - Monette's Bluff
    - Yellow Bayou

- Officers
    - Captain George W. Duncan
    - First Lieutenant George T. Hebard
    - First Lieutenant Henry N. Colburn
    - Second Lieutenant Edward Rice
    - Second Lieutenant Salmon B. Hebard

2nd Battery Light Artillery

- History
    - Mustered In
        - December 24, 1861, Brandon
    - Mustered Out
        - July 31, 1865
- Total Enrollment
    - 456 Men
- Died of Wounds
    - 1 Man
- Died in Confederate Prisons
    - 6 Men
- Died of Disease
    - 47 Men

- Organization
    - Organized at Brandon and mustered in December 24, 1861.
    - Moved to Lowell, Mass., December 24; thence to Boston February 4, 1862.
    - Embark on Steamer "Idaho" for Ship Island, La., February 6, arriving there March 8.
    - Attached to Phelps' 1st Brigade, Dept. of the Gulf, to December, 1862.
    - Artillery, 3rd Division, 19th Army Corps, Array of the Gulf, to August, 1863.
    - Garrison Artillery, Port Hudson, La., to July, 1865.

- Battles
    - Plain's Store
    - Siege of Port Hudson
    - Jackson

- Officers
    - Captain Lensie R. Sayles
    - First Lieutenant Benjamin N. Dyer
    - First Lieutenant Cordon D. Smith
    - Second Lieutenant John A. Quilty
    - Second Lieutenant John W. Chase

3rd Battery Light Artillery

- History
    - Mustered In
        - January 1, 1864, Burlington
    - Mustered Out
        - June 15, 1865

- Total Enrollment
    - 256 Men
- Died of Disease
    - 21 Men

- Organization
    - Organized at Burlington and mustered in January 1, 1864.
    - Moved to Washington, D.C., January 15-18, and duty at Camp Barry until April 5.
    - Attached to Artillery, 4th Division, 9th Army Corps, Army of the Potomac, to July, 1864.
    - Reserve Artillery, 2nd Army Corps, Army of the Potomac, to September, 1864.
    - Reserve Artillery, 6th Army Corps, and Artillery Reserve, Army of the Potomac, to June, 1865.
    - Mustered out June 15, 1862.

- Battles
    - The Crater
    - Petersburg

- Officers
    - Captain Romeo H. Start
    - First Lieutenant Roswell C. Vaughan
    - First Lieutenant Walter A. Phillips
    - Second Lieutenant John H. Wright
    - Second Lieutenant Aaron F. French

1st Cavalry

- History
    - Mustered In
        - November 19, 1861, Burlington
    - Mustered Out
        - August 9, 1865
- Total Enrollment
    - 2,304 Men
- Killed in Action
    - 72 Men
- Died of Wounds
    - 40 Men
- Died in Confederate Prisons
    - 159 Men
- Died of Disease
    - 114 Men
- Died by Accident
    - 7 Men

- Organization
    - Organized at Burlington and mustered in November 19, 1861. (Co. "L" was organized at St. Albans September 29, 1862, and Co. "M" at Burlington December 30, 1862.)
    - Left State for Washington, D.C., December 14.
    - Moved to Annapolis, Md., December 25, and duty there until March, 1862.
    - Attached to Banks' Division, Army of the Potomac, December, 1861, to March, 1862.
    - Hatch's Cavalry Brigade, Banks' 5th Army Corps, Army of the Potomac, and Dept. of the Shenandoah to June, 1862.
    - Cavalry Brigade, 2nd Army Corps, Army of Virginia, to September, 1862.
    - Price's Cavalry Brigade, Defenses of Washington, and 22nd Army Corps to April, 1863.
    - 3rd Brigade, Stahel's Cavalry Division, 22nd Army Corps, to June, 1863.
    - 1st Brigade, 3rd Division, Cavalry Corps, Army of the Potomac, to August, 1863.
    - 2nd Brigade, 3rd Division, Cavalry Corps, Army of the Potomac, to August, 1864
    - 2nd Brigade, 3rd Division, Cavalry Corps, Army of the Shenandoah, Middle Military Division, to June, 1865.

- Battles
    - Mount Jackson
    - McGaheysville
    - Middletown
    - Winchester
    - Luray Court House
    - Culpeper Court House
    - Orange Court House
    - Kelley's Ford
    - Waterloo Bridge
    - Second Bull Bun
    - Ashby's Gap
    - Aldie
    - Broad Bun
    - Greenwich
    - Warrenton
    - Hanover
    - Hunterstown
    - Gettysburg
    - Monterey
    - Leitersoille
    - Hagerstown
    - Boonsboro
    - Falling Waters
    - Port Conway

- Culpeper Court House
- Somerville Ford
- Raccoon Ford
- James City
- Brandy Station
- Gainesville
- Buckland Mills
- Falmouth
- Morton's Ford
- Mechanicsville
- Piping Tree
- Craig's Meeting House
- Spottsylvania
- Yellow Tavern
- Meadow Bridge
- Hanover Court House
- Ashland
- Hawes's Shop
- Bottom's Bridge
- White Oak Swamp
- Riddle's Shop
- Malvern Hill
- Reams's Station
- Nottoway Court House
- Roanoke Station
- Stony Creek
- Winchester
- Summit Point
- Charlestown
- Kerneysville
- Opequan
- Front Royal
- Gooney Manor Grade
- Milford
- Waynesboro
- Columbia Furnace
- Tom's Brook
- Cedar Creek
- Middle Road
- Middletown
- Lacey Springs
- Waynesboro
- Five Forks
- Scott's Corners
- Namozine Church
- Winticomack Creek
- Appomattox Station
- Appomattox Court House

- Field and Staff Officers
  - Colonel Lemuel B. Platt
  - Lieutenant Colonel George B. Kellogg
  - Major William D. Collins
  - Major John D. Bartlett
  - Surgeon George S. Gale
  - Assistant Surgeon Ptolemy O'Meara Edson
  - Adjutant Edgar Pitkin
  - Quartermaster Archibald S. Dewey
  - Chaplain John H. Woodward

- Company A
  - Captain Frank A. Platt
  - First Lieutenant Joel B. Erhardt
  - Second Lieutenant Ellis B. Edwards

- Company B
  - Captain George P. Conger
  - First Lieutenant William M. Beeman
  - Second Lieutenant Jed P. Clark

- Company C
  - Captain William Wells
  - First Lieutenant Henry M. Paige

- Company D
  - Captain Addison W. Preston
  - First Lieutenant John W. Bennett
  - Second Lieutenant William G. Cummings

- Company E
    - Captain Samuel P. Rundlett
    - First Lieutenant Andrew J. Grover
- Company G
    - Captain James A. Sheldon
    - First Lieutenant George H. Bean
    - Second Lieutenant Dennis M. Blackmer
- Company I
    - Captain Edward B. Sawyer
    - First Lieutenant Henry C. Flint
    - Second Lieutenant Josiah Grout, Jr.
- Company L
    - Captain Henry C. Parsons
    - First Lieutenant John W. Newton
    - Second Lieutenant Alexander G. Watson
- Company F
    - Captain Josiah Hall
    - Second Lieutenant Nathaniel E. Haywood
- Company H
    - Second Lieutenant Charles A. Adams
- Company K
    - Captain Franklin Moore
    - First Lieutenant John S. Ward
    - Second Lieutenant John Williamson
- Company M
    - Captain John W. Woodward
    - First Lieutenant George W. Chase

1st Infantry (Three Months)

- History
    - Mustered In
        - May 9, 1861, Rutland
    - Mustered Out
        - August 15, 1861
- Total Enrollment
    - 781 Men
- Killed in Action
    - 1 Man
- Died of Disease
    - 4 Men
- Died by Accident
    - 1 Man
- Discharged for Disability
    - 4 Men

- Organization
    - Organized at Rutland and mustered in for three months May 9, 1861.
    - Left State for Fortress Monroe, Va., May 9, arriving there May 13.
    - Camp at Hygea Hotel until May 25.
    - Demonstration on Hampton May 20.
    - Reconnoissance to Hampton May 23.
    - Occupation of Newport News May 27, and duty there until August.
    - Advance on Big Bethel June 9.
    - Moved to Brattleboro, Vt., August 4-7.

- Battles
    - Big Bethel

- Field and Staff Officers
    - Colonel John Wolcott Phelps
    - Lieutenant Colonel Peter T. Washburn
    - Major Harry N. Worthen
    - Surgeon E. K. Sanborn
    - Assistant Surgeon Willard Child
    - Adjutant Hiram Stevens
    - Quartermaster Edmund A. Morse

- Company A
    - Captain Lawrence D. Clark
    - First Lieutenant Albert B. Jewett
    - Second Lieutenant John D. Sheridan

- Company B
    - Captain William W. Pelton
    - First Lieutenant Andrew J. Dike

- Company C
    - Captain George G. Hunt
    - First Lieutenant Hiram E. Perkins
    - Second Lieutenant Freeborn E. Bell

- Company D
    - Captain Dudley K. Andross
    - First Lieutenant John B. Peckett, Jr.
    - Second Lieutenant Roswell Farnham

- Company E
    - Captain Oscar S. Tuttle
    - First Lieutenant Asaph Clark
    - Second Lieutenant Salmon Dutton

- Company G
    - Captain Joseph Bush
    - First Lieutenant William Cronan
    - Second Lieutenant Ebenezer J. Ormsbee

- Company I
    - Captain Eben S. Hayward
    - First Lieutenant Charles W. Rose
    - Second Lieutenant Orville W. Heath

- Company F
    - Captain William H. Boynton
    - First Lieutenant Charles A. Webb
    - Second Lieutenant Francis B. Gove

- Company H
    - Captain David B. Peck
    - First Lieutenant Oscar G. Mower
    - Second Lieutenant George J. Hagar

- Company K
    - Captain William Y. W. Ripley
    - First Lieutenant George T. Roberts
    - Second Lieutenant Levi G. Kingsley

2nd Infantry

- History
    - Mustered In
        - June 20, 1861, Burlington
    - Mustered Out
        - July 15, 1865
- Total Enrollment
    - 1,858 Men
- Killed in Action
    - 139 Men
- Died of Wounds
    - 84 Men
- Died in Confederate Prisons
    - 22 Men
- Died of Disease
    - 136 Men
- Died by Accident/Executed
    - 4 Men

- Organization
    - Organized at Burlington and mustered in June 20, 1861.
    - Left State for Washington, D.C., June 24.
    - Attached to Howard's Brigade, Heintzelman's Division, McDowell's Army of Northeast Virginia, to August, 1861.
    - W. F. Smith's Brigade, Division of the Potomac, to October, 1861.
    - Brook's Brigade, Smith's Division, Army of the Potomac, to March, 1862.
    - 2nd Brigade, 2nd Division, 4th Army Corps, Army of the Potomac, to May, 1862.
    - 2nd Brigade, 2nd Division, 6th Army Corps, Army of the Potomac, and Army of the Shenandoah, Middle Military Division, to July, 1865.

- Battles
    - First Bull Run
    - Lee's Mill
    - Williamsburg
    - Going's Farm
    - Savage's Station
    - White Oak Swamp
    - Crampton's Gap
    - Antietam
    - Fredericksburg
    - Marge's Heights
    - Salem Heights
    - Fredericksburg
    - Gettysburg
    - Funkstown
    - Rappahannock Station
    - Wilderness
    - Spottsylvania
    - Cold Harbor
    - Petersburg
    - Charlestown
    - Opequan
    - Winchester
    - Fiber's Hill
    - Mount Jackson
    - Cedar Creek
    - Sailor's Creek

- Field and Staff Officers
  - Colonel Henry Whiting
  - Lieutenant Colonel George J. Stannard
  - Major Charles H. Joyce
  - Surgeon Newton H. Ballou
  - Assistant Surgeon Benjamin W. Carpenter
  - Adjutant Guilford S. Ladd
  - Quartermaster Perley P. Pitkin
  - Chaplain Claudius B. Smith

- Company A
  - Captain James H. Walbridge
  - First Lieutenant Newton Stone
  - Second Lieutenant William H. Cady

- Company B
  - Captain James Hope
  - First Lieutenant Howe John
  - Second Lieutenant Enoch E. Johnson

- Company C
  - Captain Edward A. Todd
  - First Lieutenant John S. Tyler
  - Second Lieutenant Henry C. Campbell

- Company D
  - Captain Charles Dillingham
  - First Lieutenant William W. Henry
  - Second Lieutenant Charles C. Gregg

- Company E
  - Captain Richard Smith
  - First Lieutenant Lucius C. Whitney
  - Second Lieutenant Orville Bixby

- Company F
  - Captain Francis V. Randall
  - First Lieutenant Walter A. Philips
  - Second Lieutenant Horace F. Crossman

- Company G
  - Captain John T. Drew
  - First Lieutenant David L. Sharpley
  - Second Lieutenant Anson H. Weed

- Company H
  - Captain William T. Burnham
  - First Lieutenant Jerome B. Case
  - Second Lieutenant Chester K. Leach

- Company I
  - Captain Volney S. Fullam
  - First Lieutenant Sherman W. Parkhurst
  - Second Lieutenant Isaac N. Wadleigh

- Company K
  - Captain Solon Eaton
  - First Lieutenant Amasa S. Tracy
  - Second Lieutenant Jonathan M. Hoyt

3rd Infantry

- History
  - Mustered In
    - July 16, 1861, St. Johnsbury
  - Mustered Out
    - July 11, 1865
- Total Enrollment
  - 1,809 Men
- Killed in Action
  - 131 Men
- Died of Wounds
  - 65 Men
- Died in Confederate Prisons
  - 11 Men
- Died of Disease
  - 152 Men
- Died by Accident
  - 3 Men

- Organization
  - Organized at St. Johnsbury and mustered in July 16, 1861.
  - Moved to Washington, D.C., July 24-26.
  - Attached to W. F. Smith's Brigade, Division of the Potomac, to October, 1861.
  - Brook's Brigade, Smith's Division, Army of the Potomac, to March, 1862.
  - 2nd Brigade, 2nd Division, 4th Army Corps, Army of the Potomac, to May, 1862.
  - 2nd Brigade, 2nd Division, 6th Army Corps, Army of the Potomac and Army of the Shenandoah, Middle Military Division, to July, 1865.

- Battles
  - Lewinsville
  - Lee's Mills
  - Williamsburg
  - Golding's Farm
  - Savage's Station
  - White Oak Swamp
  - Crampton's Gap
  - Antietam
  - Fredericksburg
  - Marye's Heights
  - Salem Heights
  - Gettysburg
  - Funkstown
  - Rappahannock Station
  - Wilderness
  - Spottsylvania
  - Cold Harbor
  - Petersburg
  - Reams's Station
  - Ft. Stevens
  - Charlestown
  - Opequan
  - Winchester
  - Fisher's Hill
  - Cedar Creek

- Field and Staff Officers
    - Colonel William F. Smith
    - Lieutenant Colonel Breed N. Hyde
    - Major Walter W. Cochran
    - Surgeon Henry James
    - Assistant Surgeon David M. Goodwin
    - Adjutant Asa P. Blunt
    - Quartermaster Redfield Proctor
    - Chaplain Moses A. Mack

- Company A
    - Captain Wheelock G. Veazey
    - First Lieutenant Frederick Crain
    - Second Lieutenant Horace W. Floyd

- Company B
    - Captain Augustine C. West
    - First Lieutenant Enoch H. Bartlett
    - Second Lieutenant John H. Coburn

- Company C
    - Captain David T. Corbin
    - First Lieutenant Danford C. Haviland
    - Second Lieutenant Edwin M. Noyes

- Company D
    - Captain Fernando C. Harrington
    - First Lieutenant Daniel J. Kenesson
    - Second Lieutenant Charles Bishop

- Company E
    - Captain Andrew J. Blanchard
    - First Lieutenant Robert D. Whittemore
    - Second Lieutenant Burr J. Austin

- Company F
    - Captain Thomas O. Seaver
    - First Lieutenant Samuel E. Pingree
    - Second Lieutenant Edward A. Chandler

- Company G
    - Captain Lorenzo D. Allen
    - First Lieutenant John H. Hutchinson
    - Second Lieutenant Moses F. Brown

- Company H
    - Captain Thomas F. House
    - First Lieutenant Waterman F. Corey
    - Second Lieutenant Romeo H. Start

- Company I
    - Captain Thomas Nelson
    - Second Lieutenant Alexander M. Beattie

- Company K
    - First Lieutenant Amasa T. Smith
    - Second Lieutenant Alonzo E. Pearce

4th Infantry

- History
  - Mustered In
    - September 21, 1861, Brattleboro
  - Mustered Out
    - July 13, 1865
- Total Enrollment
  - 1,690 Men
- Killed in Action
  - 86 Men
- Died of Wounds
  - 73 Men
- Died in Confederate Prisons
  - 61 Men
- Died of Disease
  - 201 Men
- Died by Accident
  - 2 Men

- Organization
  - Organized at Brattleboro and mustered in September 21, 1861.
  - Moved to Washington, D.C., September 21-23.
  - Attached to Brook's Brigade, Smith's Division, Army of the Potomac, to March, 1862.
  - 2nd Brigade, 2nd Division, 4th Army Corps, Army of the Potomac, to May, 1862.
  - 2nd Brigade, 2nd Division, 6th Army Corps, Army of the Potomac, and Army of the Shenandoah, Middle Military Division, to July, 1865.

- Battles
  - Lee's Mills
  - Williamsburg
  - Gelding's Farm
  - Savage's Station
  - White Oak Swamp
  - Crampton's Gap
  - Antietam
  - Fredericksburg
  - Marge's Heights
  - Salem Heights
  - Gettysburg
  - Funkstown
  - Rappahannock Station
  - Wilderness
  - Spottsylvania
  - Cold Harbor
  - Petersburg
  - Weldon Railroad
  - Charlestown
  - Opequan
  - Winchester
  - Fisher's Hill
  - Cedar Creek

- Field and Staff Officers
  - Colonel Edwin H. Stoughton
  - Lieutenant Colonel Harry N. Worthen
  - Major John Curtis Tyler
  - Surgeon Samuel J. Allen
  - Assistant Surgeon Willard A. Child
  - Adjutant Charles B. Stoughton
  - Quartermaster John H. Cushman
  - Chaplain Salem M. Plimpton

- Company A
    - Captain John E. Pratt
    - First Lieutenant Abel K. Parsons
    - Second Lieutenant Gideon H. Burton

- Company C
    - Captain Henry B. Atherton
    - First Lieutenant George B. French
    - Second Lieutenant Daniel D. Wheeler

- Company E
    - Captain Henry L. Terry
    - First Lieutenant Stephen M. Pingree
    - Second Lieutenant Daniel Lillie

- Company G
    - Captain George P. Foster
    - First Lieutenant Henry M. Hill
    - Second Lieutenant John W. D. Carpenter

- Company I
    - Captain Leonard A. Stearns
    - First Lieutenant Levi M. Tucker
    - Second Lieutenant Albert A. Allard

- Company B
    - First Lieutenant Alfred K. Nichols

- Company D
    - Captain George Tucker
    - First Lieutenant George W. Quimby

- Company F
    - Captain Addison Brown, Jr.
    - First Lieutenant William C. Holbrook
    - Second Lieutenant Dennie W. Farr

- Company H
    - Captain Robert W. Laird
    - First Lieutenant Abial W. Fisher
    - Second Lieutenant J. Byron Brook

- Company K
    - First Lieutenant Charles W. Boutin
    - Second Lieutenant William C. Tracy

5th Infantry

- History
    - Mustered In
        - September 16, 1861 St. Albans
    - Mustered Out
        - June 29, 1865
- Total Enrollment
    - 1,618 Men
- Killed in Action
    - 136 Men
- Died of Wounds
    - 65 Men
- Died in Confederate Prisons
    - 21 Men
- Died of Disease
    - 112 Men
- Died by Accident/ Executed
    - 5 Men

- Organization
    - Organized at St, Albans and mustered in September 16, 1861.
    - Moved to Washington, D.C., September 23-25.
    - Attached to Brook's Brigade, Smith's Division, Army of the Potomac, to March, 1862.
    - 2nd Brigade, 2nd Division, 4th Army Corps. Army of the Potomac, to May, 1862.
    - 2nd Brigade, 2nd Division, 6th Army Corps, Army of the Potomac, and Army of the Shenandoah, Middle Military Division, to June, 1865.

- Battles
    - Lee's Mills
    - Williamsburg
    - Golding's Farm
    - Savage's Station
    - While Oak Swamp
    - Crampton's Gap
    - Antietam
    - Fredericksburg
    - Marye's Heights
    - Salem Heights
    - Gettysburg
    - Funkstown
    - Rappahannock Station
    - Wilderness
    - Spottsylvania
    - Cold Harbor
    - Petersburg
    - Charlestown
    - Opequan
    - Winchester
    - Fisher's Hill
    - Cedar Creek

- Field and Staff Officers
    - Colonel Henry A. Smalley
    - Lieutenant Colonel Nathan Lord, Jr.
    - Major Lewis A. Grant
    - Surgeon William P. Russell
    - Adjutant Edward M. Brown
    - Quartermaster Aldis O. Brainerd
    - Chaplain Volney M. Simons

- Company A
    - Captain Charles G. Chandler
    - First Lieutenant Alonzo B. Hurlbut
    - Second Lieutenant Louis McD. Smith

- Company C
    - Captain John D. Sheridan
    - First Lieutenant Friend H. Barney

- Company E
    - Captain Charles P. Dudley
    - First Lieutenant William H. H. Peck
    - Second Lieutenant Samuel E. Burnham

- Company G
    - Captain Benjamin R. Jenne
    - First Lieutenant Charles T. Allchinn
    - Second Lieutenant Martin J. McManus

- Company I
    - Captain John R. Lewis
    - First Lieutenant William P. Spaulding
    - Second Lieutenant Henry Ballard

- Company B
    - Captain Charles W. Rose
    - First Lieutenant Wilson D. Wright
    - Second Lieutenant Olney A. Comstock

- Company D
    - Captain Reuben C. Benton
    - First Lieutenant James W. Stiles
    - Second Lieutenant Samuel Summer, Jr.

- Company F
    - Captain Edwin S. Stowell
    - First Lieutenant Cyrus R. Crane
    - Second Lieutenant Eugene A. Hamilton

- Company H
    - Captain Charles W. Seagar
    - First Lieutenant Cornelius H. Forbes
    - Second Lieutenant Charles J. Ormsbee

- Company K
    - Captain Fred F. Gleason
    - First Lieutenant William Symons
    - Second Lieutenant George J. Hatch

6th Infantry

- History
    - Mustered In
        - October 15, 1861, Montpelier
    - Mustered Out
        - June 26, 1865
- Total Enrollment
    - 1,681 Men
- Killed in Action
    - 129 Men
- Died of Wounds
    - 60 Men
- Died in Confederate Prisons
    - 20 Men
- Died of Disease
    - 189 Men
- Died by Accident
    - 2 Men

- Organization
    - Organized at Montpelier and mustered in October 15, 1861.
    - Moved to Washington, D.C., October 19-22.
    - Attached to Brook's Brigade, Smith's Division, Army of the Potomac, to March, 1862.
    - 2nd Brigade, 2nd Division, 4th Army Corps, Army of the Potomac, to May, 1862.
    - 2nd Brigade, 2nd Division, 6th Army Corps, Army of the Potomac and Army of the Shenandoah, Middle Military Division, to June, 1865.

- Battles
    - Warwick Creek
    - Lee's Mills
    - Williamsburg
    - Golding's Farm
    - Savage's Station
    - White Oak Swamp
    - Crampton's Gap
    - Antietam
    - Fredericksburg
    - Marye's Heights
    - Salem Heights
    - Banks Ford
    - Gettysburg
    - Funkstown
    - Gainesville
    - Rappahannock Station
    - Wilderness
    - Spottsylvania
    - Cold Harbor
    - Petersburg
    - Welden Railroad
    - Reams's Station
    - Fort Stevens
    - Charlestown
    - Opequan
    - Winchester
    - Fisher's Hill
    - Cedar Creek
    - Sailor's Creek

- Field and Staff Officers
    - Colonel Nathan Lord, Jr.
    - Lieutenant Colonel Asa P. Blunt
    - Major Oscar L. Tuttle
    - Surgeon R. C. M. Woodward
    - Assistant Surgeon Charles M. Chandler
    - Adjutant Richard B. Crandall
    - Quartermaster John W. Clark
    - Chaplain Edward P. Stone

- Company A
    - Captain George Parker, Jr.
    - First Lieutenant Riley A. Bird
    - Second Lieutenant Frank G. Butterfield
- Company C
    - Captain Jesse C. Spaulding
    - First Lieutenant George C. Randall
    - Second Lieutenant Hiram A. Kimball
- Company E
    - Captain Edwin W. Barker
    - First Lieutenant Thomas R. Clark
    - Second Lieutenant Frank B. Bradbury
- Company G
    - Captain William H. H. Hall
    - First Lieutenant Alfred M. Nevins
    - Second Lieutenant Edwin C. Lewis
- Company I
    - Captain Wesley Hazelton
    - First Lieutenant William B. Reynolds
    - Second Lieutenant Edwin R. Kinney
- Company B
    - Captain Alonzo B. Hutchinson
    - First Lieutenant LaMarquis Tubbs
    - Second Lieutenant Barnard D. Fabyan
- Company D
    - Captain Oscar A. Hale
    - First Lieutenant George H. Phelps
    - Second Lieutenant Carlos W. Dwinell
- Company F
    - Captain Edwin F. Reynolds
    - First Lieutenant Elijah Whitney
    - Second Lieutenant Denison A. Raxford
- Company H
    - Captain David B. Davenport
    - First Lieutenant Robinson Templeton
    - Second Lieutenant Luther Ainsworth
- Company K
    - Captain Elisha L. Barney
    - First Lieutenant Lucius Green
    - Second Lieutenant Alfred H. Keith

7th Infantry

- History
    - Mustered In
        - February 12, 1862, Brattleboro
    - Mustered Out
        - March 14, 1866
- Total Enrollment
    - 1,572 Men
- Killed in Action
    - 2 Men
- Died of Wounds
    - 9 Men
- Died in Confederate Prisons
    - 6 Men
- Died of Disease
    - 379 Men
- Died by Accident
    - 15 Men

- Organization
    - Organized at Brattleboro and mustered in February 12, 1862, to date from June 1, 1861.
    - Left State for New York March 10, 1862.
    - Embarked March 14 for Ship Island, Miss., right wing on Steamer "Premier," and left wing on Steamer "Tamerlaine," arriving at Ship Island April 7 and 10.
    - Attached to Phelps' 1st Brigade, Dept. of the Gulf, to October, 1862.
    - District of West Florida to December, 1863.
    - Defences of New Orleans, Dept. of the Gulf, to November, 1864.
    - 2nd Brigade, Reserve Division, Dept. of the Gulf, to February, 1865.
    - 2nd Brigade, 3rd Division, 13th Army Corps, Dept. of the Gulf, to June, 1865.
    - Dept. of Texas to March, 1866.

- Battles
    - Siege of Vicksburg
    - Baton Rouge
    - Gonzales Station
    - Spanish Fort
    - Whistler

- Field and Staff Officers
    - Colonel George T. Roberts
    - Lieutenant Colonel Volney S. Fullam
    - Major William C. Holbrook
    - Surgeon Francis W. Kelly
    - Assistant Surgeon Enoch Blanchard
    - Adjutant Charles E. Parker
    - Quartermaster Edmund A. Morse
    - Chaplain Henry M. Frost

- Company A
    - Captain David B. Peck
    - First Lieutenant William L. Harris
    - Second Lieutenant Hiram B. Fish

- Company C
    - Captain Henry M. Porter
    - First Lieutenant Erwin V. N. Hitchcock
    - Second Lieutenant John Q. Dickinson

- Company E
    - Captain Daniel Landon
    - First Lieutenant George W. Sheldon
    - Second Lieutenant Richard T. Cull

- Company G
    - Captain Salmon Dutton
    - First Lieutenant George M. R. Howard
    - Second Lieutenant Leonard P. Bingham

- Company I
    - Captain Charles C. Ruggles
    - First Lieutenant Charles Clark
    - Second Lieutenant Austin E. Woodman

- Company B
    - Captain William Cronan
    - First Lieutenant Darwin A. Smalley
    - Second Lieutenant Jackson V. Parker

- Company D
    - Captain John B. Kilburn
    - First Lieutenant William B. Thrall
    - Second Lieutenant George E. Croff

- Company F
    - Captain Lorenzo D. Brooks
    - First Lieutenant Edgar N. Bullard
    - Second Lieutenant Rodney C. Gates

- Company H
    - First Lieutenant Henry H. French
    - Second Lieutenant George H. Kelley

- Company K
    - Captain David P. Barber
    - First Lieutenant John L. Mosely
    - Second Lieutenant Allen Spaulding

8th Infantry

- History
  - Mustered In
    - February 18, 1862, Brattleboro
  - Mustered Out
    - June 28, 1865
- Total Enrollment
  - 1,772 Men
- Killed in Action
  - 70 Men
- Died of Wounds
  - 32 Men
- Died in Confederate Prisons
  - 22 Men
- Died of Disease
  - 214 Men
- Died by Accident
  - 7 Men

- Organization
  - Organized at Brattleboro and mustered in February 18, 1862.
  - Left State for New York March 14.
  - Sailed for Ship Island, Miss., March 19, arriving April 6.
  - Attached to Phelps' 1st Brigade, Dept. of the Gulf, to October, 1862.
  - Weitzel's Reserve Brigade, Dept. of the Gulf, to January, 1863.
  - 2nd Brigade, 1st Division, 19th Army Corps, Dept. of the Gulf, to July, 1863.
  - 3rd Brigade, 1st Division, 19th Army Corps, to February, 1864.
  - 1st Brigade, 1st Division, 19th Army Corps, to July, 1864.
  - 2nd Brigade, 1st Division, 19th Army Corps, Army of the Shenandoah, Middle Military Division, to March, 1865.
  - 2nd Brigade, 1st Division, Army of the Shenandoah, to April, 1865.
  - 2nd Brigade, 1st Provisional Division, Army of the Shenandoah, to April, 1865.
  - 2nd Brigade, 1st Division, Defences of Washington, 22nd Corps, to June, 1865.

- Battles
  - New Orleans
  - Raceland
  - Boutte Station
  - Bayou des Allemands
  - Steamer "Cotton"
  - Bisland
  - Port Hudson
  - Opequon
  - Fisher's Hill
  - Cedar Creek
  - Newtown

- Field and Staff Officers
    - Colonel Stephen Thomas
    - Lieutenant Colonel Edward M. Brown
    - Major Charles Dillingham
    - Surgeon George F. Gale
    - Assistant Surgeon Heman H. Gillett
    - Adjutant John L. Barstow
    - Quartermaster Frederick E. Smith
    - Chaplain Francis C. Williams

- Company A
    - Captain Luman M. Grout
    - First Lieutenant Moses McFarland
    - Second Lieutenant Gilman S. Rand

- Company B
    - Captain Charles B. Childe
    - First Lieutenant Stephen F. Spaulding
    - Second Lieutenant Fred D. Butterfield

- Company C
    - Captain Henry E. Foster
    - First Lieutenant Edward B. Wright
    - Second Lieutenant Frederick J. Fuller

- Company D
    - Captain Cyrus B. Leach
    - First Lieutenant Alfred E. Getchell
    - Second Lieutenant Darius G. Child

- Company E
    - Captain Edward Hall
    - First Lieutenant Kilburn Day
    - Second Lieutenant Truman P. Kellogg

- Company F
    - Captain Hiram E. Perkins
    - First Lieutenant Daniel S. Foster
    - Second Lieutenant Carter H. Nason

- Company G
    - Captain Samuel G. P. Craig
    - First Lieutenant Job W. Green
    - Second Lieutenant John B. Mead

- Company H
    - Captain Henry F. Dutton
    - First Lieutenant Alvin B. Franklin
    - Second Lieutenant William H. H. Holton

- Company I
    - Captain William W. Lynde
    - First Lieutenant George N. Holland
    - Second Lieutenant Joshua C. Morse

- Company K
    - Captain John S. Clark
    - First Lieutenant Adoniram J. Howard
    - Second Lieutenant George F. French

9th Infantry

- History
    - Mustered In
        - July 9, 1862, Brattleboro
    - Mustered Out
        - December 1, 1865
- Total Enrollment
    - 1,878 Men
- Killed in Action
    - 13 Men
- Died of Wounds
    - 10 Men
- Died in Confederate Prisons
    - 36 Men
- Died of Disease
    - 232 Men
- Died by Accident/Suicide
    - 7 Men

- Organization
    - Organized at Brattleboro and mustered in July 9, 1862.
    - Moved to Washington, D.C., July 15-17.
    - Attached to Piatt's Brigade, Winchester, Va., to September, 1862.
    - Miles' Command, Harper's Ferry, W. Va., September, 1862.
    - Camp Douglas, Ill., to April, 1863.
    - Wardrop's Reserve Brigade, 7th Army Corps, Dept. of Virginia, to June, 1863.
    - Wistar's Independent Brigade, 7th Army Corps, to July, 1863.
    - Yorktown, Va., Dept. of Virginia and North Carolina, to October, 1863.
    - District of Beaufort, N. C., Dept. of Virginia and North Carolina, to July, 1864.
    - Defences of New Berne, N. C., Dept. of Virginia and North Carolina, to September, 1864.
    - 2nd Brigade, 2nd Division, 18th Army Corps, Army of the James, to December, 1864.
    - 2nd Brigade, 3rd Division, 24th Army Corps, Dept. of Virginia, to July, 1865.
    - 2nd Independent Brigade, 24th Army Corps, to August, 1865.
    - Dept. of Virginia to December, 1865.

- Battles
    - Harper's Ferry
    - Newport Barracks
    - Chapin's Farm
    - Fair Oaks
    - Fall of Richmond

- Field and Staff Officers
    - Colonel George J. Stannard
    - Lieutenant Colonel Dudley K. Andross
    - Major Edwin S. Stowell
    - Surgeon Benjamin Walter Carpenter
    - Assistant Surgeon Horace P. Hall
    - Adjutant John C. Stearns
    - Quartermaster Francis O. Sawyer
    - Chaplain Lucius C. Dickinson

- Company A
    - Captain Valentine G. Barney
    - First Lieutenant Linus E. Sherman
    - Second Lieutenant Erastus W. Jewett

- Company B
    - Captain Edward H. Ripley
    - First Lieutenant Samuel H. Kelley
    - Second Lieutenant Alfred C. Ballard

- Company C
    - Captain Albert R. Sabin
    - First Lieutenant Herman Seligson
    - Second Lieutenant Elijah B. Sherman

- Company D
    - Captain Charles Jarvis
    - First Lieutenant Asaph Clarke
    - Second Lieutenant Justus Dartt

- Company E
    - Captain Amasa Bartlett
    - First Lieutenant Elisha M. Quimby
    - Second Lieutenant Curtis A. Hibbard

- Company F
    - Captain George A. Beebe
    - First Lieutenant Eugene Viele
    - Second Lieutenant John T. Bascom

- Company G
    - Captain William J. Henderson
    - First Lieutenant Edwin A. Kilbourne
    - Second Lieutenant William C. Holman

- Company H
    - Captain Abiel H. Slayton
    - First Lieutenant Guy H. Guyer
    - Second Lieutenant Calvin R. Loveland

- Company I
    - Captain Albion J. Mower
    - First Lieutenant Josiah O. Livingstone
    - Second Lieutenant Oliver C. Campbell

- Company K
    - Captain David W. Lewis
    - First Lieutenant Joseph C. Brooks
    - Second Lieutenant Henry H. Rice

10th Infantry

- History
    - Mustered In
        - September 1, 1862, Brattleboro
    - Mustered Out
        - June 22, 1865
- Total Enrollment
    - 1,306 Men
- Killed in Action
    - 91 Men
- Died of Wounds
    - 58 Men
- Died in Confederate Prisons
    - 32 Men
- Died of Disease
    - 153 Men
- Discharged for Disability
    - 2 Men

- Organization
    - Organized at Brattleboro and mustered in September 1, 1862.
    - Moved to Washington, D.C., September 6-8.
    - Attached to Grover's Brigade, Military District of Washington, to February, 1863.
    - Jewett's Brigade, Provisional Division, 22nd Army Corps, Dept. of Washington, to June, 1863.
    - French's Command, 8th Army Corps, Middle Department, to July, 1863.
    - 1st Brigade, 3rd Division, 3rd Army Corps, Army of the Potomac, to March, 1864.
    - 1st Brigade, 3rd Division, 6th Army Corps, Army of the Potomac and Army of the Shenandoah, Middle Military Division, to June, 1865.

- Battles
    - Orange Grove
    - Wilderness
    - Spottsylvania
    - North Anna
    - Totopotomoy
    - Cold Harbor
    - Weldon Railroad
    - Monocacy
    - Winchester
    - Fisher's Hill
    - Cedar Creek
    - Petersburg
    - Sailor's Creek

- Field and Staff Officers
    - Colonel Albert B. Jewett
    - Lieutenant Colonel John H. Edson
    - Major William W. Henry
    - Surgeon Willard A. Child
    - Assistant Surgeon Joseph C. Rutherford
    - Adjutant Wyllys Lyman
    - Quartermaster Alonzo B. Valentine
    - Chaplain Edwin M. Haynes

- Company A
    - Captain Edwin B. Frost
    - First Lieutenant Henry H. Dewey
    - Second Lieutenant Maximillian Hopkins

- Company B
    - Captain Edwin Dillingham
    - First Lieutenant Ezra Stetson
    - Second Lieutenant Lucian D. Thompson

- Company C
    - Captain John A. Sheldon
    - First Lieutenant John A. Salsbury
    - Second Lieutenant William H. H. Sabin

- Company D
    - Captain Giles F. Appleton
    - First Lieutenant Samuel Darrah
    - Second Lieutenant George E. Davis

- Company E
    - Captain Madison E. Winslow
    - First Lieutenant Merritt Barber
    - Second Lieutenant Stephen D. Soule

- Company F
    - Captain Hiram Platt
    - First Lieutenant Chester F. Nye
    - Second Lieutenant Alexander W. Chilton

- Company G
    - Captain George B. Damon
    - First Lieutenant Pearl D. Blodgett
    - Second Lieutenant Charles G. Newton

- Company H
    - Captain Lucius T. Hunt
    - First Lieutenant Jerome C. Dow

- Company I
    - Captain Charles G. Chandler
    - First Lieutenant Charles M. Start
    - Second Lieutenant Ernest C. Colby

- Company K
    - Captain Hiram R. Steele
    - First Lieutenant Lyman C. Gale
    - Second Lieutenant Rufus K. Tabor

11th Infantry (1st Heavy Artillery)

- History (11th Infantry)
    - Mustered In
        - September 1, 1862, Brattleboro
    - Mustered Out
        - December 10, 1862

- Total Enrollment
    - 2,320 Men
- Killed in Action
    - 73 Men
- Died of Wounds
    - 79 Men

- History (1st Heavy Artillery)
    - Mustered In
        - December 10, 1862
    - Mustered Out
        - August 25, 1865

- Died in Confederate Prisons
    - 175 Men
- Died of Disease
    - 210 Men
- Died by Accident
    - 2 Men

- Organization
    - Organized at Brattleboro and mustered in as 11th Vermont Infantry September 1, 1862.
    - Left State for Washington, D.C., September 7, 1862.
    - Designation of Regiment changed to 1st Heavy Artillery December 10, 1862. (Co. "L" organized July 11, 1863, and Co. "M" October 7, 1863.)
    - Attached to 1st Brigade, Haskins' Division, Military District of Washington, to February, 1863.
    - 1st Brigade, Haskins' Division, 22nd Army Corps, Defenses of Washington, to May, 1864.
    - 2nd Brigade, 2nd Division, 6th Army Corps, Army of the Potomac, and Army of the Shenandoah, Middle Military Division, to June, 1865.
    - Middle Department, 8th Corps, to August, 1865.

- Battles
    - Spottsylvania
    - Cold Harbor
    - Petersburg
    - Weldon Railroad
    - Fort Stevens
    - Charlestown
    - Gilbert's Ford
    - Opequan
    - Fisher's Hill
    - Cedar Creek

- Field and Staff Officers
    - Colonel James M. Warner
    - Lieutenant Colonel Reuben C. Benton
    - Major George E. Chamberlin
    - Surgeon Charles W. B. Kidder
    - Assistant Surgeon Edward O. Porter
    - Adjutant Hunt W. Burrows
    - Quartermaster Alfred L. Carlton
    - Chaplain William E. Bogart

- Company A
    - Captain Edwin J. Morrill
    - First Lieutenant Edward P. Lee
    - Second Lieutenant Lester S. Richards

- Company B
    - Captain Charles Hunsdon
    - First Lieutenant Aldace F. Walker
    - Second Lieutenant Charles H. Smith

- Company C
    - Captain James T. Hyde
    - First Lieutenant William Goodrich
    - Second Lieutenant Henry S. Foote

- Company D
    - First Lieutenant Darius J. Safford
    - Second Lieutenant Charles J. Lewis

- Company E
    - Captain John Hunt
    - First Lieutenant Charles Cummings
    - Second Lieutenant John C. Sears

- Company F
    - Captain James Rice
    - First Lieutenant Nixon Morse
    - Second Lieutenant Orlo H. Austin

- Company G
    - Captain Charles Buxton
    - First Lieutenant Charles K. Fleming
    - Second Lieutenant Silas Albee

- Company H
    - Captain James D. Rich
    - Second Lieutenant James E. Eldredge

- Company I
    - Captain Robinson Templeton
    - First Lieutenant Joseph W. Leonard
    - Second Lieutenant Silas B. Tucker

- Company K
    - Captain George D. Sowles
    - First Lieutenant John R. Halbert
    - Second Lieutenant William D. Fleury

- Company L
    - Captain Darius J. Safford
    - First Lieutenant John H. Macomber
    - Second Lieutenant John S. Drenan

- Company M
    - Captain Charles K. Fleming
    - First Lieutenant Dennis Duhigg
    - Second Lieutenant Henry J. Nichols

12th Infantry (9 Months)

- History
    - Mustered In
        - October 4, 1862, Brattleboro
    - Mustered Out
        - July 14, 1863

- Total Enrollment
    - 1,005 Men
- Died of Disease
    - 63 Men

- Organization
    - Organized at Brattleboro October 4, 1862, for nine months.
    - Moved to Washington, D.C., October 7-10, 1862.
    - Attached to 2nd Brigade, Abercrombie's Division, Military District of Washington, to February, 1863.
    - 2nd Brigade, Casey's Division, 22nd Army Corps, to April, 1863.
    - 2nd Brigade, Abercrombie's Division, 22nd Corps, to July, 1863.
    - 3rd Brigade, 3rd Division, 1st Army Corps, Army of the Potomac, to muster out.

- Battles
    - Fairfax Court House
    - Gettysburg

- Field and Staff Officers
    - Colonel Asa P. Blunt
    - Lieutenant Colonel Roswell Farnham
    - Major Levi G. Kingsley
    - Surgeon Benjamin F. Ketchum
    - Assistant Surgeon Granville P. Conn
    - Adjutant Roswell C. Vaughan
    - Quartermaster Harry Brownson
    - Chaplain Lewis O. Brastow

- Company A
    - Captain Charles L. Savage
    - First Lieutenant Winslow W. Waite
    - Second Lieutenant Benjamin Warren, Jr.

- Company B
    - Captain Paul Ora, Jr.
    - First Lieutenant George L. Raymond
    - Second Lieutenant George E. Dimick

- Company C
    - Captain Lemuel W. Page
    - First Lieutenant Herman R. Wing
    - Second Lieutenant William Loomis

- Company D
    - Captain David F. Cole
    - First Lieutenant James L. Farnham
    - Second Lieutenant Henry W. Davis

- Company E
    - Captain Hamilton S. Gilbert
    - First Lieutenant George W. Robinson
    - Second Lieutenant George H. Kittredge

- Company G
    - Captain Ebenezer J. Ormsbee
    - First Lieutenant Elbridge H. Griswold
    - Second Lieutenant Lothrop J. Cloyes

- Company I
    - Captain Carlton H. Roundy
    - First Lieutenant Albert W. Russell
    - Second Lieutenant Erastus B. Tarbell

- Company F
    - Captain Darius Thomas
    - First Lieutenant James P. Cleveland, Jr.
    - Second Lieutenant Knowlton P. Howard

- Company H
    - Captain Preston S. Chamberlin
    - First Lieutenant R. E. Chamberlin
    - Second Lieutenant James W. Kelley

- Company K
    - Captain Walter C. Landon
    - First Lieutenant Stephen G. Staley
    - Second Lieutenant Edgar M. Rounds

13th Infantry (9 Months)

- History
    - Mustered In
        - October 12, 1862, Brattleboro
    - Mustered Out
        - July 21, 1863
- Total Enrollment
    - 968 Men

- Organization
    - Organized at Brattleboro October 10, 1862, for nine months.
    - Moved to Washington, D.C., October 11-13.
    - Attached to and Brigade, Abercrombie's Division, Military District of Washington, to February, 1863.
    - 2nd Brigade, Casey's Division, 22nd Army Corps, to April, 1863.
    - 2nd Brigade. Abercrombie's Division, 22nd Army Corps, to July, 1863.
    - 3rd Brigade, 3rd Division, 1st Army Corps, Army of the Potomac, July, 1863.

- Battles
    - Fairfax Court House
    - Gettysburg

- Field and Staff Officers
    - Colonel Francis V. Randall
    - Lieutenant Colonel Andrew C. Brown
    - Major Lawrence D. Clark
    - Surgeon George Nichols
    - Assistant Surgeon John B. Crandall
    - Adjutant Orloff H. Whitney
    - Quartermaster Leonard F. Aldrich
    - Chaplain Joseph Sargeant

- Killed in Action
    - 12 Men
- Died of Wounds
    - 7 Men
- Died of Disease
    - 53 Men

- Company A
    - Captain John Lonergan
    - First Lieutenant John T. Sinnott
    - Second Lieutenant David McDevitt

- Company B
    - Captain Orcas C. Wilder
    - First Lieutenant Nathaniel Jones, Jr.
    - Second Lieutenant Clesson R. McElroy

- Company C
    - Captain Lewis L. Coburn
    - First Lieutenant George S. Robinson
    - Second Lieutenant William E. Martin

- Company E
    - Captain Joseph J. Boynton
    - First Lieutenant Andrew J. Davis
    - Second Lieutenant Frank Kenfield

- Company G
    - Captain Marvin White
    - First Lieutenant Merritt B. Williams
    - Second Lieutenant Nelson Goodspeed

- Company I
    - Captain John M. Thatcher
    - First Lieutenant Charles E. Bancroft
    - Second Lieutenant James S. Peck

- Company D
    - Captain William D. Munson
    - First Lieutenant George Bascom
    - Second Lieutenant John M. Rolfe

- Company F
    - Captain John L. Yale
    - First Lieutenant Lucius H. Bostwick
    - Second Lieutenant Justin Naramore

- Company H
    - Captain William V. Peck
    - First Lieutenant Aro P. Slayton
    - Second Lieutenant Hiram Perkins

- Company K
    - Captain George G. Blake
    - First Lieutenant Stephen F. Brown
    - Second Lieutenant Carmi L. Marsh

14th Infantry (9 Months)

- History
    - Mustered In
        - October 21, 1862, Brattleboro
    - Mustered Out
        - July 30, 1863
- Total Enrollment
    - 964 Men
- Killed in Action
    - 18 Men
- Died of Wounds
    - 9 Men
- Died in Confederate Prisons
    - 2 Men
- Died of Disease
    - 39 Men

- Organization
    - Organized at Brattleboro October 21, 1862, for nine months.
    - Moved to Washington, D.C., October 22-25.
    - Attached to 2nd Brigade, Abercrombie's Division, Military District of Washington, to February, 1863.
    - 2nd Brigade, Casey's Division, 22nd Army Corps, to April, 1863.
    - 2nd Brigade, Abercrombie's Division, 22nd Army Corps, to July, 1863.
    - 3rd Brigade, 3rd Division, 1st Army Corps, Army of the Potomac, to muster out.

- Battles
    - Fairfax Court House
    - Gettysburg

- Field and Staff Officers
    - Colonel William T. Nichols
    - Lieutenant Colonel Charles W. Rose
    - Major Nathaniel B. Hall
    - Surgeon Edwin H. Sprague
    - Assistant Surgeon Lucretius D. Ross
    - Adjutant Harrison Prindle
    - Quartermaster Charles Field
    - Chaplain William S. Smart

- Company A
    - Captain Ransom O. Gore
    - First Lieutenant Edward N. Thayer
    - Second Lieutenant Charles Albro
- Company B
    - Captain John C. Thompson
    - First Lieutenant Adoniram J. Blakely

- Company C
    - Captain Josiah B. Munson
    - First Lieutenant Nathan L. Andrew
    - Second Lieutenant Henry D. Young
- Company E
    - Captain Edwin Rich
    - First Lieutenant Henry B. Needham
    - Second Lieutenant Andrew J. Child
- Company G
    - Captain Noble F. Dunshee
    - First Lieutenant John H. Allen
    - Second Lieutenant Charles W. Mason
- Company I
    - Captain Solomon T. Allen
    - First Lieutenant T. C. Middlebrook
    - Second Lieutenant Milo A. Williams
- Company D
    - Captain Charles E. Abell
    - First Lieutenant John W. Woodruff
    - Second Lieutenant Don Juan Wright
- Company F
    - Captain Joseph Jennings
    - First Lieutenant Julius H. Bosworth
    - Second Lieutenant Charles A. Rann
- Company H
    - Captain Walter C. Dunton
    - First Lieutenant Alanda W. Clarke
    - Second Lieutenant Daniel Conway
- Company K
    - Captain Alonzo N. Colvin
    - First Lieutenant William H. Munn
    - Second Lieutenant Lewis P. Fuller

15th Infantry (9 Months)

- History
    - Mustered In
        - October 22, 1862, Brattleboro
    - Mustered Out
        - August 5, 1863

- Total Enrollment
    - 942 Men
- Died of Wounds
    - 78 Men
- Suicide
    - 1 Man

- Organization
    - Organized at Brattleboro and mustered in October 22, 1862, for nine months.
    - Moved to Washington, D.C., October 23-26.
    - Attached to 2nd Brigade, Abercrombie's Division, Military District of Washington, to February, 1863.
    - 2nd Brigade, Casey's Division, 22nd Army Corps, to April, 1863.
    - 2nd Brigade, Abercrombie's Division, 22nd Army Corps, to June, 1863.
    - 3rd Brigade, 3rd Division, 1st Army Corps, Army of the Potomac, to muster out.

- Battles
    - Fairfax Court House
    - Catlett's Station
    - Gettysburg

- Field and Staff Officers
    - Colonel Redfield Proctor
    - Lieutenant Colonel William W. Grout
    - Major Charles F. Spaulding
    - Surgeon Carlton P. Frost
    - Assistant Surgeon Gates B. Bullard
    - Adjutant Joseph M. Poland
    - Quartermaster Putman D. McMillian
    - Chaplain Ephraim C. Cummings

- Company A
    - Captain Horace E. Brown
    - First Lieutenant William H. Norton
    - Second Lieutenant Luman V. Quimby

- Company B
    - Captain James M. Ayer
    - First Lieutenant Lucius S. Gerry
    - Second Lieutenant John B. Rogers

- Company C
    - Captain Cornelius N. Carpenter
    - First Lieutenant Marshall A. Carpenter
    - Second Lieutenant Edward E. Herrick

- Company E
    - Captain Warren Noyes
    - First Lieutenant Joseph S. Hall
    - Second Lieutenant Robert P. Noyes

- Company G
    - Captain Stephen R. McGaffey
    - First Lieutenant George H. Blake
    - Second Lieutenant Stephen O. Elkins

- Company I
    - Captain William H. Johnston
    - First Lieutenant Freeman F. Bean
    - Second Lieutenant William M. Tibbetts

- Company D
    - Captain Charles G. French
    - First Lieutenant Harry Downing
    - Second Lieutenant Warren C. Meserve

- Company F
    - Captain Xerxes C. Stevens
    - First Lieutenant John C. Blanchard
    - Second Lieutenant Moses Lyman, Jr.

- Company H
    - Captain Riley E. Wright
    - First Lieutenant John H. Oakes
    - Second Lieutenant Rufus Averill

- Company K
    - Captain George B. Woodward
    - First Lieutenant William A. Chapman
    - Second Lieutenant John R. Thompson

16th Infantry (9 Months)

- History
  - Mustered In
    - October 23, 1862, Brattleboro
  - Mustered Out
    - August 10, 1863
- Total Enrollment
  - 968 Men
- Killed in Action
  - 16 Men
- Died of Wounds
  - 8 Men
- Died in Confederate Prisons
  - 1 Man
- Died of Disease
  - 48 Men

- Organization
  - Organized at Brattleboro and mustered in October 23, 1862, for nine months.
  - Moved to Washington, D.C., October 24-27.
  - Attached to 2nd Brigade, Abercrombie's Division, Military District of Washington, to February, 1863.
  - 2nd Brigade, Casey's Division, 22nd Army Corps, to April, 1863.
  - 2nd Brigade, Abercrombie's Division, 22nd Army Corps, to June, 1863.
  - 3rd Brigade, 3rd Division, 1st Army Corps, Army of the Potomac, July, 1863.

- Battles
  - Burke's Station
  - Catlett's Station
  - Gettysburg

- Field and Staff Officers
  - Colonel Wheelock G. Veazey
  - Lieutenant Colonel Charles Cummings
  - Major William Rounds
  - Surgeon Castanus B. Park, Jr.
  - Assistant Surgeon George Spafford
  - Adjutant Jabez D. Bridgman
  - Quartermaster James G. Henry
  - Chaplain Alonzo Webster

- Company A
  - Captain Henry A. Eaton
  - First Lieutenant Daniel M. Clough
  - Second Lieutenant Joseph W. Waldo
- Company B
  - Captain Robert B. Arms
  - First Lieutenant John F. Vinton
  - Second Lieutenant Charles A. Norcross

- Company C
    - Captain William H. Walker
    - First Lieutenant Asa G. Foster
    - Second Lieutenant Luther F. Moore
- Company E
    - Captain Alvin C. Mason
    - First Lieutenant Joseph Spafford
    - Second Lieutenant Warren E. Williams
- Company G
    - Captain Harvey N. Bruce
    - First Lieutenant Benjamin C. Dutton
    - Second Lieutenant Francis C. Clark
- Company I
    - Captain Lyman E. Knapp
    - First Lieutenant Kettredge Haskins
    - Second Lieutenant Ira W. Thomas
- Company D
    - Captain David Ball
    - First Lieutenant Charles E. Goodhue
    - Second Lieutenant Oscar W. Sherwin
- Company F
    - Captain Henry F. Dix
    - First Lieutenant Henry O. Gillett
    - Second Lieutenant George H. Burns
- Company H
    - Captain Joseph C. Sawyer
    - First Lieutenant Elmer D. Keyes
    - Second Lieutenant John C. Sanborn
- Company K
    - Captain Samuel Hutchinson
    - First Lieutenant Lewis Graham
    - Second Lieutenant William Danforth

17th Infantry

- History
    - Mustered In
        - April 12, 1864, Brattleboro
    - Mustered Out
        - July 14, 1865
- Total Enrollment
    - 1,106 Men
- Killed in Action
    - 72 Men

- Died of Wounds
    - 61 Men
- Died in Confederate Prisons
    - 33 Men
- Died of Disease
    - 57 Men
- Died by Accident
    - 3 Men

- Organization
    - Organized and mustered in: Companies "A" January 5, 1864; "B," "C" and "D" March, 1864; "E," "F" and "G" April 12, 1864.
    - Moved to Alexandria, Va., April 18-22, 1864.
    - Attached to 2nd Brigade, 2nd Division, 9th Army Corps, Army of the Potomac, to July, 1865.

- Battles
    - Wilderness
    - Spottsylvania
    - North Anna
    - Totopolomoy
    - Bethesda Church
    - Cold Harbor
    - Petersburg
    - The Crater
    - Weldon Railroad
    - Poplar Spring Church
    - Hatcher's Run

- Field and Staff Officers
    - Colonel Francis V. Randall
    - Lieutenant Colonel Charles Cummings
    - Major William B. Reynolds
    - Surgeon Ptolemy O'Meara Edson
    - Assistant Surgeon Henry Spohn
    - Adjutant James S. Peck
    - Quartermaster Buel J. Derby

- Company A
    - Captain Stephen F. Brown

- Company B
    - Captain Andrew J. Davis
    - First Lieutenant Edward L. Hibbard
    - Second Lieutenant Alonzo H. Danforth

- Company C
    - Captain Frank Kenfield
    - First Lieutenant Guy H. Guyer
    - Second Lieutenant Charles W. Randall
- Company E
    - Captain George S. Robinson
    - First Lieutenant William E. Martin
    - Second Lieutenant William B. Burbank
- Company G
    - Captain Eldin J. Hartshorn
    - First Lieutenant Leonard P. Bingham
    - Second Lieutenant Charles D. Brainard
- Company I
    - Captain Daniel Conway
    - First Lieutenant William H. Norton
    - Second Lieutenant George W. Tobin
- Company D
    - Captain Henry A. Eaton
    - First Lieutenant Gardner W. Gibson
    - Second Lieutenant Worthington Pierce
- Company F
    - Captain Lyman E. Knapp
    - First Lieutenant George Hicks
    - Second Lieutenant George W. Kingsbury
- Company H
    - Captain Charles M. Corey
    - First Lieutenant Henry B. Needham
    - Second Lieutenant John R. Converse
- Company K
    - Captain John C. Yale
    - First Lieutenant Arnold C. Fay
    - Second Lieutenant J. E. Henry

18th Infantry

Organization Not Complete

BIBLIOGRAPHY

Alexander Street Press, LLC. "The American Civil War Research Database." Alexander Street Press. asp6new.alexanderstreet.com/cwdb/ (accessed September 4, 2013).

Dyer, Frederick H. *A Compendium of the War of the Rebellion*. New York: T. Yoseloff, 1959.

Fox, William F. *Regimental Losses in the American Civil War, 1861-1865 a treatise on the extent and nature of the mortuary losses in the Union Regiments, with full and exhaustive statistics compiled from the official records on file in the state military bureaus and at W*. Fourth Edition ed. Albany: Albany Pub. Co., 1898.

Official Army Register of the Volunteer Force of the United States Army for the years 1861, '62, '63, '64, '65. Washington, D.C.: Adjutant General's Office, 1865.

Peck, Theodore S. *Revised roster of Vermont Volunteers and lists of Vermonters who Served in the Army and Navy of the United States during the war of the rebellion, 1861-66*. Montpelier: Press of the Watchman Pubshing Co., Publishers and Printers, 1892.

The Union Army: A History of Military Affairs in the Loyal States 1861-65. Madison, Wis.: Frederal Publishing Company, 1908.

CPSIA information can be obtained
at www.ICGtesting.com
Printed in the USA
LVHW060837241020
669716LV00045B/2457

9 781492 818762